the WOODS
the SEA
pluff MUD
and ME

DANNY WILLCUTT

the WOODS the SEA pluff MUD and ME

Poems About Nature on the
South Carolina Coast

Charleston, SC
www.PalmettoPublishing.com

The Woods, The Sea, Pluff Mud, and Me

Copyright © 2023 by Danny Willcutt

All rights reserved

No portion of this book may be reproduced, stored in a retrieval system, or transmitted in any form by any means—electronic, mechanical, photocopy, recording, or other—except for brief quotations in printed reviews, without prior permission of the author.

First Edition

Paperback ISBN: 979-8-8229-2053-8

Contents

Edisto: 174	1
Tides	2
Hurricane	3
Damn Hot Charleston Summer	4
Broken Seashell	5
Edisto Rainbow	6
Big Fat Squirrel	7
Milky Way from Edisto	9
Oak Tree	10
Edisto Sunrise	11
The White Crane	12
Edisto Time	13
Ocean	14
Shrimp Boat of Big Bay Creek	16
My Little Farm	17
Dirt Road	18
Campfire	19
Toogoodoo Fireflies	21
Pelican	23
When the Woods Awake	24
Crabbing on the Creek	25
Baby Sea Turtle	26
First Fish	27
Rainy Days	28
Carolina Winter	29
Old Tire Swing	31
Spiderweb	32
Are We Here Alone?	33
Red Bird	34
Moonlight on the River	35
Shooting Star	36
The River	37
Your Happy Place	38
Red-Headed Woodpecker	39
Fog on the Beach	40

Morning Drive 42
Edisto Starfish 44
Clamshell 45
The Red-Tailed Hawk .46
Carolina Wren 47
Corn/Survive 48
Poisoned By Pluff Mud 50
Squirrel Fight 51
Heaven's Beach 52
Write Your Troubles in the Sand 53
The Morris Island Lighthouse 54
Neighbors' Rooster 55
Where the Fox Squirrels Play 56
Flat Squirrel 57
Butterfly 58
Lightning 59
Beauty in the Woods .60
The Old Fox and the Young Fox 61
Reflection Returns 62
The Gate 63
Edisto Sunset 64
Sweet Magnolia 65
Crabbing 66
Big Cat 67
Music of the Marsh 69
Watching It Rain 70
Egret on a Gator Ride 71
Alligator 72
Morning Sky 73
Woodland Bandit 74
Turtle on a Four Lane 75
The Blue Heron 76
Between the Sea and Me 77
It's Alive/Living Shell .78
Shapes in the Clouds .80
Shell Tree 81
Armadillo 82

Blackbirds 84
Sharks 85
Roseate Spoonbill 87
Tree Frog 88
Beach Forever Gone (Erosion) 89
Evenings on the Farm 91
Beach Chair 92
The Storm's Not Over Yet 93
Seagulls 95
Clearing Land 96
Power of Water 98
The Beauty of Broken Things 99
Frosty Beach 100

Edisto: 174

There exists to me this special place,
Where the sea meets Heaven's floor;
Its path is found beneath oaks,
At the end of 174.

I've been blessed for most my life
To live close to its shore;
It's there I find my solitude,
At the end of 174.

I feel that in a past life,
I've lived it here before,
And God so chose to send me back
To the end of 174.

Maybe when I leave this life
And I draw my breath no more,
I pray they spread my ashes
At the end of 174.

Tides

The tide comes in,
The tide goes out
It changes every day.

What's not been seen
In a thousand years
Is quickly washed away.

What once was there
But now is gone
May someday come again.

Or find its place
On a distant shore
When the tide comes washing in.

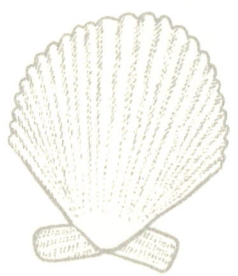

Hurricane

The clouds they darken far offshore,
And the sun, it fades away.
I know in time the sun will leave,
As the darkness fills the day.

The wind will come, the waves will pitch,
Eating all that's in its way.
What once stood strong, but now is gone,
Leaves nothing left to say.

Almost every summer,
When the ocean starts to boil,
It leaves us coastal dwellers
With hours lost in toil.

What to take and what to leave,
Which windows should I board?
Early to the store we go,
Before the masses start to hoard.

We pray until it's past
To see how much still stands
And look upon the aftermath
At all the shifted sands.

Those who've never seen it
May think it's no big deal,
But you will never know the feeling,
Until it's yours to feel.

If you think it cannot happen,
The past reveals a chill.
Read a little history
Of a place called Edingsville.

Damn Hot Charleston Summer

Never quite sure what to wear,
This weather is a bummer,
But one thing you can count on
Is a damn hot Charleston summer.

Mosquitoes big as mockingbirds,
Horseflies bite like flames,
Snakes of different sizes,
Both with and without fangs.

The sun is out, no call for rain,
But that will never last;
Wait ten minutes and it will change,
Once the thunderstorm rolls past.

If we had separate seasons,
I'm sure that would be nice,
But we seem to get all seasons
In one big humid slice.

Yes, I choose to live here—
Thank God I'm not a runner,
'Cause no one ever gets use to
This damn hot Charleston summer.

Broken Seashell

I picked up a little seashell,
And I went to throw it back;
It was rough around the edges,
And the center had a crack.

It seemed it had a hard life,
Had seen its better days;
It showed a life of turmoil,
Being rolled around by waves.

No promise for the future,
With no luster to be shown,
No one would want this ugly shell,
When its beauty is now gone.

So, as I went to throw it,
The thought occurred to me,
I'm a bit just like this seashell—
We are all broke to some degree.

Life's not always easy;
I've got my share of scars—
I'm rough around the edges,
But I've gotten pretty far.

Like that little seashell,
What the outside did reveal
Reminds me of me,
So, it now lives up on my windowsill.

Edisto Rainbow

As I walk in total solitude,
With the sand beneath my feet,
Searching for the treasures
Left by the waves' retreat.

Just north of the inlet,
With no shelter to be found,
I see the storm clouds forming
And lightning touch the ground.

A little fear comes over me
As to how I will get back;
My throat tightens a little
As the lightning starts to crack.

But as the storm moves past
And the sun returns to glow,
The beauty of the sky
Reveals a bright rainbow.

I've always known the blessing
Of living close to this place,
And I feel the calm come over me,
As the sunlight touches my face.

In a moment I start to realize
Just where my fortunes lay,
It's found along its beaches,
Its creeks, its sounds, and bays.

I'm not sure about the pot of gold
Or what the folklore does bestow,
But the ending of the rainbow
Is found on Edisto.

Big Fat Squirrel

My wife comes home from the grocery store
With all the bags she stowed.
The fat squirrel sits up on a limb
And inspects what she unloads.

He searches for the birdseed,
Then he preps his midnight ride.
Like Paul Revere, with his squirrel voice clear,
He notifies his tribe.

They stalk until the moment's right,
Like a ninja on attack.
With little greedy eyes they watch;
They're just looking for a snack.

They climb and slide, back down the pole,
Where the feeder sits up top,
Relentless in their quest for seeds,
So never will they stop.

They gather at the bottom,
Like a herd of hungry beasts,
All waiting for the one up top
To shake the feed and start the feast.

Now the fat squirrel's at the bottom,
'Cause he cannot climb the pole,
But it seems that he's the one in charge,
Like a greedy little troll.

He runs away the other squirrels
As often as he can,
But he knows soon he needs their help—
This is all his master plan.

When the fat squirrel's finished eating,
He's as full as he can be
And must now rely on the other squirrels
For a boost to climb the tree.

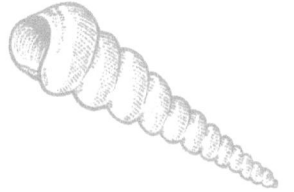

Milky Way from Edisto

Sun is down, moon's not yet up,
But the sky is on display,
The wonders of the universe,
Seen through the Milky Way.

The gentle breeze blows through the trees,
The marsh grass starts to sway,
Nighttime starts to settle in,
As the night birds start to play.

Sitting on this dock tonight
Has me feeling kind of small;
The wonders of my little world
Are not so small at all.

I gaze in wonder at the sky,
Like millions have before,
Amazed at all the beauty
That circles heaven's door.

I'm grateful for the sights I see
That some have never seen;
The life I'm living in this place
Most would call it a dream.

I pray I never leave from here,
Till the Lord calls me away,
And then will be my time at last
To pass through the Milky Way.

Oak Tree

You were just a baby
A hundred years before my birth;
You could live a hundred more,
After I leave this earth.

You stood and watched the storms roll past—
You've even weathered war;
I think of all the things you've seen
As history passed your door.

I used to climb your branches;
I've rested 'neath your shade.
When it comes to other animals,
Think of all the homes you've made.

But the times they are a-changin,
With destruction caused by man,
All portrayed as greater good,
Reaps scars upon the land.

Just a few apartments,
A couple more strip malls;
Where once was just a forest,
No trees now stand at all.

Will you make it through development
Or be lost to greed and plans?
Nothings ever sacred
Beneath footprints of man.

I hope you're still around
To be seen by my child's child,
So maybe she can rest, like me,
Beneath your shade a while.

Edisto Sunrise

Ever watched the sun come up
Across the Carolina shore?
The blessing of a brand-new day,
Of which we are never sure.

The sky, it seems, is all on fire,
With reds of different shades,
And a little orange tossed right in,
To balance the cascade.

The sun comes out the water,
And the beach starts to awake.
The little creatures scurry 'round,
Chased in and out by wakes.

The seagulls and the pelicans
Once again take flight,
After resting on the ocean waves,
Just waiting for daylight.

The sunrise seams to offer up
What all have waited for:
A chance to start another day
Upon this blessed shore.

A chance for me to get it right,
To be better than yesterday.
A chance to earn the blessing
And see the sunrise one more day.

The White Crane

The white crane wades the water
In the shallows of the lake;
Statue still with its long bill,
It waits for a mistake.

A shallow swimming little fish,
A tree frog on a reed,
A crawfish gets a little close,
And the white crane shows its speed.

Nature's poetry in motion—
It's in almost every beast.
Everything's a hunter,
And everything's a feast.

It's the nature of all nature;
Something lives and something dies.
It sounds a bit barbaric,
But it's how the wild survives.

A fox waits by the shoreline,
Near the shallows of the lake,
Statue still with all his skill,
As the crane makes its mistake.

Beneath the lake the gator waits,
As still as any stone,
Waiting for the fox to jump,
And the cycle goes on and on.

Edisto Time

No one's in a hurry here,
No special place to go.
Seems it has its own time zone,
This place called Edisto.

Basics in the grocery store,
But it's really all you seek.
A little seasoning here and there;
The rest you catch in the creek.

Got to love the mornings here:
No six-lane traffic ride.
Everything you want to do
Is all controlled by tide.

For the early bird, the morning sun
Shows magic for the eyes,
But the night owls here are not left out
When the sunset paints the skies.

It's a special kind of atmosphere,
An aura in this place.
Life here doesn't run on norms;
It runs at its own pace.

It's a laid-back sort of feeling,
Once you cross the Dahoo River.
Most places seem to take from life,
But Edisto is a giver.

Ocean

What treasures lie beneath your waves?
What mysteries do you hold?
Your bounty feeds all nations,
But your secrets are rarely told.

I've seen you on your calm days;
I've seen your anger roll.
And many lives have been lost
When you decide to take your toll.

No one will ever tame you,
Although many often try.
It's only those, of whom you choose,
That you truly let pass by.

Things that live beneath your crest,
Allowed to call you home,
Some never seen by the eyes of man.
Some will always be unknown.

As I walk along this seashore
And take all the glory in,
It's easy to get overwhelmed
By the beauty with no akin.

We blast off into outer space,
Because we just can't go that deep
To discover what's still here on earth
And what lies that far beneath.

Imagine all that we could see
If we could roll the water back.
Treasures from the start of time
Now rest in cold and black.

I think I've found my treasure here,
And it lies not far beneath:
It's the sights and sounds, from where I stand,
With the sand under my feet.

Shrimp Boat of Big Bay Creek

The shrimp boat leaves from Big Bay Creek
At the south of Edisto.
Way before the sun comes up,
You can see the mast lights glow.

Slowly out to sea she goes,
To the shrimping grounds offshore,
In hopes to get its cooler full,
'Cause that's its daily chore.

Some days are good; some days are not.
It's the way that shrimping goes;
It's the kind of work that's in your blood,
As every shrimper knows.

At nighttime you can see their lights
If you're walking down the beach,
Underneath the star filled sky,
Working till the limit's reached.

Some days they make a profit;
Some days don't pay for fuel.
Though its sounds somewhat romantic,
Some days are downright cruel.

Escorted back by seagulls
Swooping down to make a snatch
From the shrimp heads going overboard,
As the crew heads out their catch.

But today the crew seems happy
As they come back to the creek,
Maybe 'cause they're loaded
Or because they get the chance to sleep.

My Little Farm

I wake up in the morning,
After cursing the alarm,
Off and to the real world,
Far from my little farm.

Driving down the driveway,
You never know quite what you'll see,
Across the ditch and past the pond,
Through a narrow spot of trees.

Eyes glowing in the headlights,
From all the critters and the deer,
Everything is safe from harm,
'Cause there's nothing here to fear.

Always something broken,
The chore list is immense,
But it seems I'm never happier
When moving dirt or fixing a fence.

At nighttime you can walk outside
And the sky is crystal clear;
No city lights distort the view
Of the heavens from out here.

I've still got years of driving left,
Going to and from this place,
But one day if my plan is sound,
I'll escape from the rat race.

Then morning time will find me
Drinking coffee at the barn,
Loving every minute spent
Down on my little farm.

Dirt Road

Oak tree limbs that arch the road,
As if reaching for each other,
Like children playing games outside,
As they dance with one another.

Branches draped in Spanish moss,
Just swaying with the breeze—
Feels like autumn setting in,
As it whispers through the trees.

Dragonfly zips down the road,
Stopping now and then to rest,
But he doesn't stay in one place long,
'Cause the next place might be best.

Birds are singing happy songs,
Sunlight filters through the leaves,
Wildflowers growing everywhere,
Like they were planted just for me.

I could walk for hours here,
Just soaking up the sights.
Sometimes it's just the simple things
That makes things seem all right.

Life can overpower you
If you give it half a chance.
Sometime a dirt road walk can help
And not let things advance.

A time to think things over
Can reduce a heavy load.
I think sometimes this is why
God gave us a dirt road.

Campfire

There's something about a campfire
That's a mesmerizing sight.
I could watch for hours,
As the flames dance in the night.

It flickers and it flutters,
Changing colors now and then.
Sparks rise up into the air,
Then they go back out again.

A relaxing kind of feeling,
When friends are gathered 'round,
But it's okay if you're by yourself,
Alone there on the ground.

I love to watch the smoke rise up
And watch the embers glow;
It's almost like it draws you in,
As it's putting on a show.

Maybe cook a little dinner,
Maybe drink a couple beers,
Maybe just sit back and clear your head,
Because stress is not found here.

Telling stories with your friend around
That get bigger as time goes on,
Or recalling an old memory
That gets sweeter when you're alone.

There's something about a campfire
That's just soothing to your mind,
A peaceful kind of feeling
That lets your soul unwind.

Yup, there's something about a campfire
That lets you toss your troubles in
And watch them all go up in smoke
And scatter to the wind.

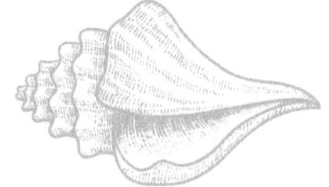

Toogoodoo Fireflies

There's a special treat, around our farm,
From May to mid-July:
Fireflies start to reappear
All through the nighttime sky.

It starts with just a few at first,
Then it's like they're everywhere,
Like Christmas lights, but all in white—
Must be thousands in the air.

We used to walk around the yard,
Catching them in mason jars,
Then take them back into the house,
And watch them glow like stars.

We would keep them for a little while,
And then we'd set them free
To watch them fly back to the woods,
Where all their friends would be.

It's a special part of growing up,
In a special kind of place,
No city lights to dim the glow
Of the smile on a child's face.

As the little firefly stops to rest,
Upon their outstretched arm,
Then flies away into the night,
Across our little farm.

And just as fast, they're gone at last,
Like they all dropped from the sky,
And seldom are they seen again,
Until winter passes by.

But I know next year, they will return,
From May to mid-July,
And we're blessed to have this little farm,
When the fireflies start to fly.

Pelican

Not sure that it's supposed to fly,
But it moves with grace across the sky,
A prehistoric looking bird,
The pelican's built somewhat absurd.

They dive like bombers from way up high
And pounce the fish that are swimming by.
They get their fill with just one bite,
Then they float a while till their next flight.

No matter what the weather's like,
They're always there, and quite a sight,
Whether perched upon a pylon post
Or leisure cruising down the coast.

They fly formation down the beach,
Until their destination is reached.
Just be very careful if you're beneath,
'Cause the bombs they drop can cause you grief.

Not many things are so unique
As a pelican with its great big beak.
Of all the creatures along the coast,
This bird's the one that I like the most.

If you have a chance to rest a while
On a beach near some deserted isle,
I'm sure you'll see this graceful beast,
As it makes its clumsy dive to feast.

When the Woods Awake

If long before the light of day
You creep down in the woods a ways,
You never know quite what you'll see,
If you go in as quiet as you can be.

The noise you hear when the woods awake
Is almost more than you can take.
It seems that every beast makes sounds
From in the trees and on the ground.

As the nighttime things head off to bed
And the daytime things awake instead,
Their paths all cross down in the woods—
You're in the wildlife's neighborhood.

Like people on a busy street,
Some heading to work, some home to sleep,
Their lives converge the same as ours,
Just like it does during our rush hour.

The sun comes up and it starts to change,
The animals split up and rearrange.
What roams at night is now asleep,
And the daytime things all start to creep.

But when the sun starts sinking low,
The animals all know where to go—
Some off to bed, some off to roam,
With all that call the woods their home.

Crabbing on the Creek

The most fun thing I ever did,
When I was just a little kid,
Was crabbing from a salt creek bank
And waiting for my string to yank.

With a chicken neck tied to a string,
In hopes the crab would bite and cling,
Tossed in the creek with our little bait,
Sunk to the bottom while we would sit and wait.

But you wouldn't be there very long:
The string would move, and the game was on
To slowly pull that blue crab in
Before it turned loose and was gone again.

Sometimes it took us several tries
To pull from the creek our little prize,
To get the crab close enough to shore
And scoop again with our net once more.

Then home we'd go to cook our catch,
Playing with the claws, in a sword fight match.
We would eat and talk about our day,
Remembering the ones that got away.

Turns out my kids are just like me
When it comes to crabbing down on the creek.
I hope they remember the fun we had,
Like I remember crabbing with their granddad.

Baby Sea Turtle

One little baby turtle, crawling down the sand,
Heading toward the ocean, trying to leave the land,
Left by all the others because it hatched too late,
Never really knowing what would be its fate.

Hatched beneath the surface, then digging itself out,
Had planned to hit the surf and then to travel south.
If it's lucky to get past the waves, and then on out to sea,
Maybe it will stand a chance if the fish will let it be.

It spends its whole life growing up trying not to be a meal,
For all the other creatures the ocean does conceal.
So many miles it travels, through the oceans of this earth,
In hopes to make its way back to the beach from which it birthed.

Many years of swimming around, then finally it returns,
Back to the Carolina shore, where its instinct truly yearns,
To lay a nest of loggerheads and then return to sea,
In hopes the eggs will all hatch out when it's their time to leave.

The tide is right, the full moon shines, the eggs they hatch at last,
And all the little turtles crawl toward the sea so fast.
But one little baby turtle it seems has missed the date,
Left by all the others because it hatched too late.

Then all alone, with fate unknown, it finally makes it out,
Across the sand and to the surf, with plans of heading south.
Just like its mom did years ago, it heads out all alone,
Till years from now it will return, to lay a nest here of its own.

First Fish

It's like a rite of passage
From somewhere in your past,
A memory that lives on with you,
The kind that always lasts.

Someone special takes you fishing—
There's always your first time.
All the first-time things you do
Tend to stay there in your mind.

Just a cricket and a cane pole,
Down at an old farm pond
Or maybe at the ocean—
It all depends on where you're from.

The excitement from a youngster,
From the tugging of the line—
Nothing can replace the feeling
Of catching fish for the first time.

If you're older there's the feeling
That you've learned how to survive.
No matter what comes after this,
You can keep yourself alive.

The Bible says to give a fish,
You feed someone for the day,
But take the time to teach them how
And they survive along the way.

No matter what's the lesson,
The smile just says it all.
The first time that you catch a fish
Makes you feel at least ten feet tall.

Rainy Days

I remember well when growing up
The days the rain would fall,
Stuck there in the house alone,
With no fun to have at all.

Nothing's worse than how you felt
On a cold and rainy day,
When all you'd want is just the chance
To go outside and play.

Face pressed against the windowpane,
With nothing more to do
Than sit and watch the raindrops fall,
Like it's there to punish you.

Praying it would go away
Just seemed to make it worse.
For a kid that's trapped inside all day,
It's somewhat of a curse.

I'm older now, and my thoughts have changed
When it comes to rainy days—
A chance to stop and rest a while
And clear the mental haze.

But I remember how it felt back then,
When the thunder begins to call,
As my child stares out the windowpane,
And the raindrops start to fall.

Carolina Winter

We don't have a lot of winter,
Along the Carolina shore,
Compared to other places,
Where the snow can block your door.

In fact, the change of season
At times is hard to see.
It's usually pretty normal
To be kind of warm on New Year's Eve.

But when the frost first comes around
And things turn icy white,
You got to love the things you see,
Just as it turns daylight.

The rivers have an eerie mist,
The marsh grass has a glaze,
And as the sun is coming up,
There's a coolness in its rays.

The marsh hens screech their normal sounds,
The seagulls squawk in flight,
Like they're talking to each other,
Saying it was cold last night.

The farmhouse just back off the road
Has its chimney belching smoke;
It swirls around and back to the ground
And then filters through the oaks.

You can see the horse's breath come out
From across the frosty pasture;
It could be a scene in a country dream
Any artist would want to capture.

It can't be hot here all the time,
And we all like a change in weather,
Just as long as it don't stay too long,
Because our flip flops are our treasure.

Old Tire Swing

Of all the things found around the farm,
A tire swing seems to have the most charm.

It's like a fixture that's supposed to be
Hanging from the branch of a big oak tree.

Just a piece of rope and an old car tire
Are the only things that are required.

A place where children learn to play
Or where young lovers plan out their day.

Where the older folks can remember when
And walk down memory lane again.

It's a place that makes the dreamers dream
Or a simple place just to ponder things.

No need to have a reason why,
Just swing a while and let time pass by.

In life you outgrow a lot of things,
But you never outgrow an old tire swing.

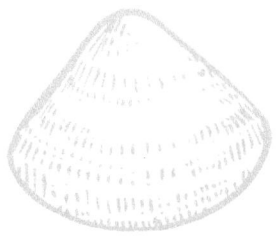

Spiderweb

You can see it in the distance,
Just swaying in the breeze;
It wasn't there the day before,
Stretched between the trees.

It glistens with the morning dew,
This amazing piece of art.
This tiny little creature
Must be an engineer at heart.

It works all day and most the night,
As it spins its great big web,
In hopes to catch its dinner soon
So its little ones are fed.

How does it know which way to go,
When tying all those knots?
But it makes sure that everything
Is tied off in the right spots.

It's amazing to see how nature works
And how things live their lives;
Each creature does its little part,
As it works to stay alive.

It's survival of the fittest,
But that's always nature's way;
Its only job is to figure out
Just how to outsmart its prey.

But this tiny little spider,
With the beautiful web it weaved,
Has figured out just how to sit
And wait for dinner to be received.

Are We Here Alone?

Have you ever looked up at the sky,
On a clear and starry night,
And wondered if we're the only ones
God made with all his might?

Is it far-fetched to think that God
Would have created other worlds
In a distant far-off universe,
With his own hands he hurled?

At times you see a distant star
Or a shimmering-colored light;
Do you ever stop to think that it
Could be a rocket ship in flight?

Just because it is not mentioned
In the Bible that we read,
If we believe that God can do all things,
Then to this we must concede.

I wonder if they are just like us
Or maybe much more advanced.
Could they have learned how not to hate
So the universe still has a chance?

Red Bird

They say to see a red bird
Is a sign from up above,
A symbol from the other side,
From someone that you love.

A message on a pair of wings,
A sign you'll be okay,
Just a little bit of encouragement
To help you through the day.

An angel watching over you
Till you're together once again,
A reminder that you're not alone
As you carry them within.

No one ever truly leaves
When you hold their memory dear,
For while they live within your heart,
They will always be right here.

It hurts when someone leaves this earth;
There's a void that can't be filled,
And nothing can replace them,
And there's no one that ever will.

But in the times we're feeling lonely
And not sure how to carry on,
Don't be surprised if you look outside
And a red bird comes along.

Moonlight on the River

There is nothing quite as beautiful
As the full moon on the river;
The ripples on the water's edge
Appear to make it quiver.

Reflecting like a mirror,
The full moon way up high
On the surface of the water,
As the tide goes washing by,

Hung there like a picture frame,
Way up in the winter sky,
Playing peek-a-boo throughout the night,
As the clouds are floating by.

Seen as strength and power
By some who gaze above,
But often called the lover's moon,
As lovers fall in love.

However that it makes you feel,
You just can't deny the pull
From all the force that is produced
From when the moon is full.

So, marvel in the wondrous sites
The full moon does provide,
And feel the awesome power
As your thoughts drift with the tide.

Shooting Star

Some say that it's a good luck thing,
Some say it means disaster.
I guess it's just what you believe
In the beliefs of which you master.

You look up at a star-filled night,
And it shoots across the sky,
Like a white-hot glowing ember,
With a tail as it goes by.

Never quite sure what it is,
As they're really very fast,
You only get a glimpse of them
As they are streaking past.

They say that's it's a dying star
That's burning itself out,
But are we ever really sure,
Or do we have our doubts?

I wonder where it's coming from
Or where it's going to;
Could it be some sort of rocket ship
That's just coming into view?

I guess we'll never know for sure
Just what they really are,
But all my life I've always heard,
"Wish upon a shooting star."

So, when you see a shooting star
On a night that's crystal clear,
Don't forget to close your eyes and wish,
But just pray it don't land here.

The River

The river is like a magnet
That sort of pulls you in,
A place that draws your deepest thoughts,
As it flows around the bend.

The peacefulness of watching it
Is healing for your soul,
A place to cast your troubles in—
The things you can't control.

A place to sit for hours,
Where you never do get bored.
There's always so much going on,
As it flows between the shores.

It's like it speaks a language
That's know by everyone;
It's like it understands you,
No matter where you're from.

To sit down by the river
As it flows out toward the sea
Is truly one of the simple things
That helps to set you free

From all life's little problems
That rear their ugly head
And try to overpower you,
With all the things you dread.

So, find yourself a river
If you search for peace of mind;
It will help to soothe your troubles,
As you watch the river wind.

Your Happy Place

For everyone it's different,
The place they feel their best,
A place that brings their soul alive
And puts their mind at rest.

That place for me is often found
In many different forms,
And each one may not be the same,
But each has memories worn.

I love the beach at Edisto,
Where the salt spray hits my face.
You can truly see the wonders there
That God so chose to grace.

Not far from here is an old dirt lane,
Where the oak trees arch the road.
The peace I feel when walking here
Helps my mind to just unload.

The rivers flow out to the sea
And bring all forms of life;
No better place to sit a while
When your life is full of strife.

I've seen the mountains way up high;
I've seen the valleys low;
I've seen the brilliant summer skies
God's hand chose to bestow.

You see, to find your happy place
Is not that hard to do;
It's any place that brings you peace,
Like it was put there just for you.

Red-Headed Woodpecker

The big red-headed woodpecker,
Clinging to the tree,
Beats his head against the bark
To see what he can see.

A big old bug or tasty grub
Is what he's searching for.
Looking for a tasty snack,
He pecks a little more.

What a way to make a living,
What a way to just survive:
To beat your head against a tree,
Just to stay alive.

I've seen him work for hours,
Just banging with his beak.
I'm glad it's not my line of work
And it's not grubs I seek.

On second thought, I think I know
Sort of how he feels.
Each day I work and rack my brain
To just bring home the meals.

At least I do not spend my day
Going from tree to tree
And beat my head against the bark,
So that's just fine by me.

Fog on the Beach

It's the eeriest of feelings
When walking down the beach
On a cold crisp winter morning,
With the sand beneath your feet.

You see the fog roll on to shore,
Then the gray spreads all about
As a solid misty wall appears
That blocks the ocean out.

It sometimes stops at shoreline;
Sometimes it comes ashore;
Sometimes it moves right over you,
Like some spooky old folklore.

It's crazy how your mind will run
When you're in this situation,
Remembering all the ghostly tales
Told by your past relations.

The feelings that come over you
When you cannot see a thing
Make you think the kind of things
You never wished to think.

Could it be the souls that have been lost?
Did the sea give up her dead?
Or is it my time to leave this earth,
And it comes for me instead?

It's a little bit unnerving,
Even for a full-grown man,
To disappear within the fog
When you're walking across the sand.

If it's my time to leave this world
When the fog rolls off the sea,
At least I'll be right where I love
And in good company

Morning Drive

I wake up in the morning,
Giving thanks I'm still alive,
Then I hop into my pickup truck
And make my morning drive.

Mindless down the highway,
I think of all that I must do,
Then I see a bit of sunrise
As it's coming into view.

Most days the sun is coming up
As I cross the river bend;
It creeps up out the ocean
And pushes nighttime to its end.

The nighttime and the daytime,
Both fight to take control,
But the sun will win this first round
As the night begins to fold.

The rays of gold and amber
Go streaking across the sky,
Like it's telling all God's creatures,
It's a great day to be alive.

Nothing's such a blessing
As to see another day,
A gift that others didn't get
When their last was yesterday.

Treat this blessing with respect
That a new day is really worth,
For it may be the last day
We walk upon the earth.

Darkness wins the round tonight
As the sun begins to fade,
But the sun will rise tomorrow
And fight the dark for another day.

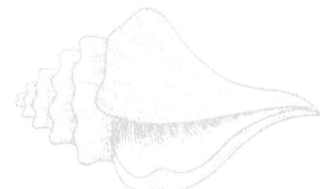

Edisto Starfish

Been cold here now at least a week,
With frosting on the beach.
The stars they have descended
And now lie within our reach.

Hundreds lying everywhere—
I guess too cold to fly—
Twinkle, twinkle, little star,
I can't just pass you by.

Too cold to crawl back to the sea,
And they will never last the tide.
Life is getting shorter
With every moment that goes by.

I pick them up and toss them back
Into the ocean waves,
In hopes they will revive themselves
And live another day.

No way that I can save them all—
Some are too far gone—
But maybe I can save a few
As I just walk along.

I know they're not the stars we see
When we gaze up at the sky,
But maybe the starfish we throw back
Will someday learn to fly.

Clamshell

A hundred years of hiding,
Buried 'neath the mud and sand,
A clamshell washed by a hurricane
Far out away from land.

Hidden beneath the ocean waves,
Seems like forever and a day,
Then washed back by another storm
To the beach where it now lays.

A little girl picks up this shell
And carries it back home
And puts it with her other shells,
But now at least it's not alone.

One day she goes back to the pile
And picks up the shell again.
"What a lovely ornament this would make,"
As she stands there with a grin.

With a little paint and a little string,
The shell's now on display
With all the other ornaments
As they wait for Christmas day.

As the years go by, this old clamshell
Hangs on many trees
As it makes its way throughout the years,
Passed down by the family.

Each year the story's always told,
"Great-great-grandma made this when
She was only ten years old,
With a shell she found back then."

The Red-Tailed Hawk

The red-tailed hawk is soaring,
High up in the air,
Just drifting on an ocean breeze,
Like a feather floating there.

So effortless he glides right past,
Then his screech says he's arrived.
He's waiting for his prey to move,
Then he makes his deadly dive.

Folded up and straight down to earth,
He zips right through the trees.
He grabs his quest, puffs out his chest,
Then flies back through the leaves.

His dinner for tonight it seems
Never had a clue
Today would be its final day,
When the hawk came soaring through.

Both marvelous and deadly
Are the birds of prey.
Never killing just for fun,
They just try and make their way.

With watchful eye he soars up high,
Seeing everything below.
A mouse, a snake, or fish in the lake
Never sees him sweeping low.

Such a beautiful part of nature,
With his skills all on display,
So mystical and graceful,
Where on the breeze he chooses to play.

Carolina Wren

Not certain why this pesky bird
Has got it in its mind
That's it's okay to build its nest
Wherever it can find.

Underneath your car hood,
Beside the front porch light,
Or even in your pair of boots
When left out overnight.

Lots of trees and bushes—
In fact, acres that it could use—
But it seems to have its heart set on
The place we must refuse.

We've parked the bikes for weeks on end,
Due to nests built in the baskets,
And even ceased to use the grill,
'Cause of their aggravating tactics.

It breaks my heart to watch it,
As it works without a rest,
Then I must try and relocate,
Because of where it built its nest.

Every spring they start right back—
It happens year after year—
You'd think one day they'd get the point
And just not build them here.

It's such a pretty, little bird,
The Carolina wren,
But it's such a stubborn little thing,
As it builds its nest again.

Corn/Survive

I wonder just how many folks
Would know where to get corn.
If not bought from the grocery store,
Just where on earth's it born?

How to grow a little seed
And watch it break the soil,
By mixing love and water,
Applied with a bit of toil.

The people who can't catch a fish
Or raise a chicken egg,
What would you do if up to you—
Would you be reduced to beg?

If you had to feed your family
With just your own two hands,
How many folks would starve to death
If forced to live from off the land?

If all life's great conveniences
Were to suddenly go away,
And no longer was there an internet,
Would you just go astray?

We like to take for granted
Our way of life will always be—
No need to know such petty things;
Plenty's always a guarantee.

But remember throughout history,
Empires rise and empires fall;
The pharaohs and the Mayan kings
Were of the first to lose it all.

So, learn self-preservation,
While you still have a chance
To watch your YouTube videos
And learn from those who can.

Poisoned By Pluff Mud

When I was very young,
I got this strange disease;
I guess it got into my blood
As I sank up to my knees.

Dad took me to get oysters,
Picked them right up off the bank.
This gooey stuff was everywhere,
And into my heart it sank.

I've been fortunate to live my life
Along the rivers, creeks, and bays
Of the Carolina shoreline,
Where I've spent most of my days.

I'm happy to have traveled
Across this country and abroad,
But it's here the pluff mud calls to me
With a voice that's never flawed.

So, if you've been so afflicted,
I can tell you there's no cure.
Take it from me, it will always be
Within your blood, rest assured.

Squirrel Fight

Squirrel fight at the feeder—
Someone's going down.
The little squirrel is finally tired
Of being pushed around.

He balls his fist up tightly,
With an acorn in each hand,
No plan of backing down again—
This time he's got a plan.

The big squirrel at the bottom
Is denying him the chance
To eat the feed that's in the feeder;
He takes up a defying stance.

Too long he's been a bully
To all the other squirrels.
Today he finally meets his match
When they all decide to quarrel.

Now the big squirrel thinks he's got this—
He is bigger than the little guy—
But he fails to see the other squirrels
That are lurking real close by.

So today the tide is finally turned,
And the big squirrel runs away,
Pounded by the acorns
All the little squirrels threw his way.

The moral of the story
Is the food you need to share,
Because all the crafty little squirrels
Have now learned to fight in pairs.

Heaven's Beach

If God decides to call me home
While I'm walking down this beach,
That would be just fine with me—
The angels won't have far to reach.

It there's a heaven here on earth,
It's the beach at Edisto,
The place that makes my spirit soar
And where blessings overflow.

My mind is never more at peace
Than when I'm at this place;
It's easy to see God's handiwork,
And you will surely feel his grace.

The power of the ocean waves
And the painted skies above,
The simple way it gets to you—
You can't help but fall in love.

Whether here for fifteen minutes
Or hanging out for days,
This place can speak straight to your heart;
Nature's best is on display.

So, if my final day is to be found
On the beach at Edisto,
I bet the angels will all draw straws
To see who gets to go.

Write Your Troubles in the Sand

Write your troubles in the sand,
And watch them wash away,
As the waves take them back out to sea
And let them drift off where they may.

Each day the tide will rise and fall,
Moving on and off the shore.
Everything that once was here
Is now gone forevermore.

We must learn to just let go
Of things that haunt our past.
We can only carry strife so long,
Or we are never going to last.

The burden that our thoughts can place
Upon our fragile heart
Can dim our light that shines within
And change what we impart.

We cannot expect forgiveness
From those that won't forgive,
So we cannot be expected
To waste the time we live.

So, find yourself a beach somewhere,
And write your troubles in the sand.
Watch the waves devour them
And wash them from your hands.

The Morris Island Lighthouse

Back before technology
Was strapped upon our wrist,
The simple stars were all we used
To guide us through the mist.

Then a distant light from far away
Would take us in to shore.
That beacon on a stormy night
Was welcoming for sure.

While most it brought home safely,
Others died within her sight,
Never setting foot upon the land
She marked for them that night.

A tall and slender lighthouse,
To so many, the saving grace,
The image of an angel
In an unforgiving place.

Standing guard just like a sentry,
Calling sailors home once more,
She promised them safe harbor
It they could navigate her shore.

She's now just a reminder
Of long-forgotten days,
Replaced by other gadgets
That helps lost sailors find their way.

She still stands at Morris Island,
Though she stands in disrepair,
But occasionally they light her lamp,
So her beauty we once more share.

Neighbors' Rooster

My neighbors got a rooster
That must have lost its sight.
It's supposed to crow at 6:00 a.m.,
But the dang thing crows all night.

You can hear him in the morning
And throughout the afternoon
And at night while you are sleeping—
You'd think he'd wear out soon.

But he never seems to be too tired
To let us know that he's awake.
His crowing is soon to reach a point
That I can no longer take.

I love my life out on the farm,
But there are things I wouldn't miss,
Like waking up throughout the night,
Because this thing disrupts my bliss.

Last night I finally got some sleep,
Because I believe that he's been stricken.
So, if you're hungry come on by my place,
We'll be having some fried chicken.

Where the Fox Squirrels Play

Hidden 'neath the mighty oaks
At a place called Botany Bay
Is a winding dirt road through the woods,
Where the fox squirrels come to play.

Shadows filled with mystery,
An image of bygone days,
First know to horse and wagon
Is where the fox squirrels come to play.

It takes you back into a time
Of plantations and soirees,
A mix of good and bad events,
Where the fox squirrels come to play.

This road has seen so many things,
With some history of dismay,
But lessons from the past can teach,
Where the fox squirrels come to play.

This peaceful place I first did see
When in my youthful phase;
The place that I still love to walk
Is where the fox squirrels come to play.

So, if you ever take that scenic drive,
Slowly passing by this way,
Maybe you can catch a glimpse
As the fox squirrels come out to play.

Flat Squirrel

The road is full of flat squirrels
That could not make up their mind
To simply just turn right or left,
Until they ran right out of time.

Standing on the highway,
They see the danger coming close
But stuck there in the moment,
When it really counted most.

Whether blinded by the headlights
Or mesmerized by sounds,
No matter what the reason,
The direction could not be found.

The same is true in all of us
When we face uncertain times:
Sometimes we simply take too long
To just make up our mind.

Its best to pay attention
When things in life don't coincide
And not just let things happen
When our time comes to decide.

The moral of the story?
Problems will not just erode;
Take action to resolve them,
And don't be the flat squirrel on the road.

Butterfly

How wonderful is nature
In the way it brings forth life?
What once was just an ugly worm
Is now a butterfly in flight.

A symbol of tranquility,
Of beauty, peace, and grace,
It flutters on the morning breeze,
As it goes from place to place.

They come in many colors,
But mostly yellow, black, and green,
But then flies by the Monarch,
With a mixture of everything.

You can chase them 'round for hours,
And they are just out of your reach,
But then they'll land right on your shoulder
As you're just walking down the beach.

A signal from this wondrous place
That spring's almost arrived,
And soon the springtime showers
Will have everything revived.

The woods will bring forth its new life,
With all the birds and bees,
But nothing is more beautiful
Than the butterflies on the breeze.

Lightning

The sky is black, no stars that shine,
But there's a rumble in the distance.
Then suddenly you see a flash,
As the lightning shows persistence.

Streaking out across the sky,
With all types of jagged shapes,
Trying to predict how far
By the sound the thunder makes.

It's a mesmerizing sight to see,
And you just can't help but feel
As if it wants to draw you in,
Like it's got you on a reel.

Rolling out across the sea,
Far out from the beach,
It's really putting on a show,
And we pray we're not in reach.

So beautiful it is to watch,
But you must respect the power:
It can turn the night into the day,
And all your senses it devours.

Its nature's way of showing off,
But one thing I'm thankful for:
I glad I'm watching it from here
And not on the fishing boat offshore.

Beauty in the Woods

In the woods, the beauty's found
In almost everything,
From the sound made by the bumble bee
To the way the songbirds sing.

The rustle in the treetops,
As the gray squirrels run around,
And the crunching of the dried-up leaves,
As the racoons search the ground.

The flowers of the dogwood tree
And honeysuckles on a fence,
The wild azaleas all in bloom
Make the fragrance seem intense.

Little doe is munching grass
At the corner of the field.
As the filtered rays of sunlight stream,
It seems that heaven is revealed.

A hawk is screeching overhead,
And a dragonfly is out to play,
And all the other signs of life
Go on about their day.

I walk along and take it in.
All of life, it seems quite good
When you just take time to soak it up,
From the beauty found in the woods.

The Old Fox and the Young Fox

The old fox and the young fox,
Standing just inside the woods,
Scoping out the hen house
That's holding all the goods.

Young fox licks his lips and says,
Old man, you best wait here.
I'll bring us back a chicken
Before they even knew I was there.

Old fox tells the young fox,
Son, you best slow yourself down.
Don't be in such a hurry now—
The farmers are still around.

But the young fox is impatient.
Seeing the chicken he wants to steal,
He heads off to the hen house
In hopes to grab a meal.

But halfway across the open field,
The farmer's rifle plays its part.
The young fox starts to realize
Maybe he's not so smart.

He makes it back into the woods,
Where the old fox shakes his head.
He says, Son, you're too impatient—
You should have listened to what I said.

The old fox tells the young fox,
There was a lesson learned today.
If you want to live to be my age,
You must learn some patience along the way.

Reflection Returns

Skipping rocks across the pond,
Making ripples as it touches down
And shatters the reflection of
The peacefulness all around.

The ripples work their way across
The surface of the pond,
Until they reach the far-off edge,
Then the reflection calmly responds.

Such is true in all of life:
There are things that cause a ripple
And distort the beauty we perceive
And change what seems so simple.

Given time the wake will cease,
Then the surface turns to glass
And returns to show reflections of
The things that are meant to last.

Give some time for things to pass;
Let the ripples settle down,
And you will find things will return
To reflect the peacefulness all around.

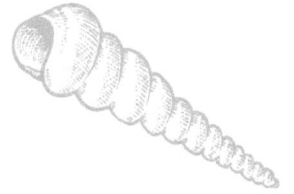

The Gate

The simple rules of farm boy
All revolve around the gate.
The first of every lesson learned
Is of this simple bit of fate.

Like leave it as you find it
Is the best bit of advice.
If you want to piss a farm boy off,
Make him say this twice.

No matter what the weather—
It's not up for debate—
The youngest one inside the truck
Gets out to get the gate.

This system starts off early,
I guess around two or three;
As soon as you could reach the latch,
It became your job, you see.

At one time it was kind of fun—
It made you feel grown up—
But now you're just the gofer
For everyone else in the truck.

No need to try and argue;
You were just born a little late.
Until a younger rider comes along,
Just get out and get the gate.

Edisto Sunset

The sun heads toward the water
At the ending of the day;
It kind of paints a portrait
In the sky across the bay.

The brilliant red and orange,
Mixed with every shade of blue,
Painted by the hand of God—
It is such a lovely view.

You can hear it as it sizzles
In the water just offshore,
As slowly it's extinguished,
Until the day returns once more.

Its task is done for one more day,
As it brought its warmth and light,
And now it has a chance to rest,
As the day turns into night.

Tomorrow it will come again,
And if I'm so blessed to go,
I'll watch the sun set one more time
From the beach at Edisto.

Sweet Magnolia

All across the southland,
Where the groceries grow in rows,
That's where I choose to live my life,
Where the sweet magnolias grow.

Where the creeks are full of wildlife,
And to the ocean is where they flow,
It's where I grew to be a man
And where the sweet magnolias grow.

The place I've raised my family
And watched my children grow,
Where most our memories have been made,
From where the sweet magnolias grow.

A place where every afternoon
The sunset is quite a show—
It's just like heaven here on earth,
Where the sweet magnolias grow.

At night you see a million stars,
A sight some will never know.
No better place that I have found
Than where the sweet magnolias grow.

Where life runs at a slower pace
And where people still say hello
When they see you walking down the street—
It's where the sweet magnolias grow.

I pray that God will grant to me
One last request, before I go,
Just let me spend my final days
Where the sweet magnolias grow.

Crabbing

Brightly painted milk jugs
Up and down the creek,
With the crab pots at the bottom—
Carolina blue is what they seek.

The big and tasty blue crab
That live along these parts—
You even see them on the wall
Of someone's painted art.

The crabber at his daily grind,
Just harvesting his catch,
With great big bushel baskets,
Then they sell them as a batch.

The hours long, the work is hard—
Nothing easy about this job—
And what you put your body through
Makes every muscle throb.

The type of work that you must love,
That makes you get up in the morning
And launch your boat despite the news
Of issued small-craft warnings.

A tough way to make a living,
Along the Carolina shore,
But the view there from the office
Makes it worth the daily chore.

Big Cat

They say it's nonexistent,
That it died out long ago,
But I can tell you for a fact
Their fact just isn't so.

I've seen it cross the woodland road;
I've seen its telltale signs;
I've heard it in the morning hours—
It sends a chill right up your spine.

The Carolina panther,
A big black majestic beast
That lurks within the shadows,
And in the shadows is where it feasts.

They used to have a place to hide,
Far out of human sight,
But with all the trees we're cutting down,
Staying hid is a growing fight.

I've hunted, fished, and walked this place,
Been in these woods for many years,
And I've only seen them once or twice
In all the time that I've been here.

They are the stealthiest of creatures,
Which is why they're still around.
In the day they're in the treetops,
But at night they're on the ground.

Just because you have not seen it
Doesn't mean that it's not so.
This big cat really does live here,
Though rarely does it show.

So, if you see a flash of black go by
Or hear it scream in predawn hours,
It's likely not to bother you,
If there's something else there to devour.

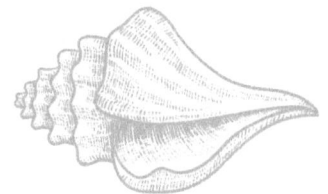

Music of the Marsh

Marsh grass makes a scratchy noise
As it sways with the gentle breeze.
The tide laps at the oyster bank,
Then it flows out to the sea.

The dolphins play out in the creek,
Chasing fish up close to shore,
Feeding in the shallow wake—
There must be three or four.

The marsh hens make their clucking sound,
The seagulls make their squawk,
The fiddler crabs move up the bank,
With their sideways walk.

On the bank the shorebirds run around,
Making sounds like pops and clicks,
Their long beaks pecking at the mud—
They look like big farm chicks.

An outboard makes its rumbling sound
As the cab boat moves on past.
He pulls his pots from out the creek,
And by the seagulls he's harassed.

All these sounds merge into one
To play its heartfelt song.
The music of the marsh it's called,
And all the creatures sing along.

Watching It Rain

The sun slept in this morning,
'Cause the clouds keep hanging 'round.
I guess it needs a little rest
As this rain is coming down.

Maybe I should stay in bed,
Get myself some extra sleep,
But my mind's programed for 5:00 a.m.,
And my thoughts are running deep.

Wonder what I'll do today
Within this soggy mess.
My list of chores is getting long,
But with rain they won't get addressed.

So many things that need repair
Here on my little farm,
But I guess if it goes one more day,
It will not cause us any harm.

I had things to do, but that's okay—
No need to just complain.
So, I'll just sink myself into this chair,
Drink coffee and watch it rain.

Egret on a Gator Ride

The egret's out in the water,
And it's standing kind of tall
On the back of an alligator,
Like he has no brain at all.

A little snap and that's all she wrote,
And the egret would be gone,
But that don't seem to bother him,
As he just rides on along.

The alligator doesn't seem to care
That he's got a ride-along;
He's soaking up a little warmth,
Before the evening sun is gone.

The next time out, it might not be
The egret that is the winner,
But lucky for this crazy bird,
This gator already had his dinner.

So, ride along, you trusting bird,
But please don't turn your back,
Because tomorrow just may be the day
This alligator wants a snack.

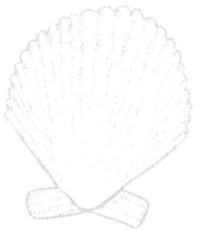

Alligator

The most prehistoric beast on earth
Is lying up on the sand,
Trying to get a little sun,
Like he's working on his tan.

He's laid up on the golf course,
But they are really everywhere.
A river, lake, or shady pond—
You will likely find one there.

They lurk there in the shallows—
They love to feast on fish,
But anything that gets too close
Can become a tasty dish.

They are quiet as a church mouse,
Lying at the water's edge
Or sometimes on a riverbank,
High up on a ledge.

They outlived all the dinosaurs,
And they learned how to adapt,
But they look so peaceful lying there
In the sunshine taking naps.

But don't trust this big, majestic beast,
And don't get too close to look.
Remember from your nursery rhymes,
Or you'll end up like Captain Hook.

Morning Sky

As I drive to work each morning
And see the clouds formed just offshore,
They look like mountain ranges
That go on forevermore.

Like hills, and peaks, and valleys,
Looks like the image of a ghost,
'Cause no way they could be mountains,
Here off the Carolina coast.

With every color of the rainbow,
It is painted across the sky,
The beauty reeks of inspiration
As I just drive on by.

So lucky that I am to see
The glory of this day,
All the wonders of creation
Right up there on display.

It's sights like this that help to calm
All the troubles in your mind.
It lets you gather a little peace,
If even just for a short time.

It really is the little things
That get us through the day,
A chance for us to still our thoughts
And smile a little along the way.

Woodland Bandit

The bandit of the woodland
Comes complete with built-in mask,
And going through your trash can
Is the racoon's nightly task.

It's a furry little creature
That's mostly out at night
But sometimes in the daytime,
If there is food within its sight.

Such pesky little critters,
Although they're cute enough
You almost want to overlook
The fact they tear up stuff.

They are sneaky and resourceful,
And they mostly live in trees,
But they are likely to just build their nest
Any dang where that they please.

They have their way to figure out
Anything they want to do,
And they take great pride in proving
They can easily outsmart you.

They have their little work-arounds—
They are much smarter than you think.
Just when you think you've shut them out,
They are back inside before you blink.

So don't be surprised to hear a noise
In your attic late one night;
It's just the racoon babies,
Turning on and off the light.

Turtle on a Four Lane

Turtle on a four lane,
Trying to make his way across.
With all it owns strapped to its back,
This could be its biggest loss.

He starts off at the white line,
Runs to the center of the lane
And tucks his head into his shell.
Until the cars pass, he remains.

He sticks his head back out his shell,
Looks around, then off he goes,
To the center of the next lane,
Until the traffic starts to flow.

I swear I think he's got a plan—
It's like he's done this all before.
He waits until the cars pass by,
Then he runs a little more.

So, I'm feeling sorry for him
And pull over so I can help,
But this crazy little turtle
Has made the trip all by himself.

I'm really happy for him—
He made it just like that,
But the irony here is to be found
In a rabbit that's squashed flat.

The Blue Heron

Blue heron creeping around the pond,
Like a soldier on patrol,
Searching for a tasty treat,
While he takes his morning stroll.

Around the pond and through the grass,
In and out the tall cattails,
Picking off the little fish,
But he could likely eat a whale.

So quietly he walks around,
You can barely see him move;
With total concentration,
You can tell he's in his groove.

His every step has style and grace,
Like a dancer at a ball,
Yet every step at a deadly pace,
And no fish are safe at all.

He will stay a while and then fly off,
But he will be back this afternoon,
Searching for another treat,
When his timing is opportune.

Between the Sea and Me

There are times when contemplating
How the things in life should be,
I find my deepest conversations
Take place between the sea and me.

Sometimes I walk for hours—
God's creation is what I seek—
And I feel the closest to his grace
When it's just the sea and me.

You may think I'm talking to myself,
But when you're closer you will see
I'm simply lost in observations,
Just between the sea and me.

At times I've found some answers
That have brought me to my knees,
With no form of hesitation
There between the sea and me.

I come to ponder over things,
'Cause the future is not foreseen.
It's always helped to calm my mind,
Talks between the sea and me.

One day I'll have no further questions,
And my ashes will drift free,
Then there will be no separation
Between the sea and me.

It's Alive/Living Shell

For weeks I've searched around the sea,
Hoping to find the perfect shell.
Finally, there it was at last,
By the rocks when the tide fell.

I've only been here to the sea
Maybe just once or twice.
To take with me a souvenir,
That surely would be nice.

I reach through the wave and pick it up
And see something there inside—
Some type of creature has my shell
And there chosen to reside.

Who would know, if just this once
I keep this little shell,
Even if it's occupied
By some creature I can't expel?

The beauty of this little shell
Would look great up on my mantel.
Inside my home far from the beach,
It would be a great example.

Of all the wonders of the earth
That live along the sea,
I don't think any harm would come
If this one went home with me.

But as I look down at this shell,
My heart so plainly sees
This is such a precious thing,
And maybe I should set it free.

I gently place it back onto
The sand where it came from,
And one day if I do come back,
I'll see how big it has become.

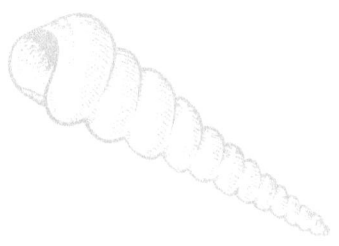

Shapes in the Clouds

I lie back on an afternoon
And gaze up at the sky,
Watching all the fluffy clouds
As they go drifting by.

The vapor trail from airplanes,
Mixed with birds that fly around,
Enhances everything I see
From down here on the ground.

Like the picture someone shows to you
That messes with your senses,
An ugly hag at first you see,
But then she changes to princess.

The clouds to me are much the same
As I pick out the different shapes.
It may not look the same to you,
Because this is my escape.

All the cotton candy colors
Mixed with streaking rays of sun,
Making shapes up in the clouds
That looks like something or someone.

Some would call it lazy,
Just a total waste of time,
But picking shapes out of the clouds
Is a feeling that's so sublime.

It's said daydreaming's good for you,
A real relaxing thing to do.
So, I think I'll lie right here a while
And watch the clouds as they drift through.

Shell Tree

Washed off a tiny island
By a tide that was extreme,
Out near the mouth of Big Bay Creek
On a day the sea was mean.

The old dead tree with branches bare
Just drifted with the tide,
Then one day came to rest upon
The beach on the other side.

An ugly thing with no leaves of green,
Stranded high up on the sand,
Waiting for the next king tide
To wash it out again.

But as it waited for the tide,
Something wonderful began to show:
Folks would hang their seashells there
And say a prayer for those they know.

For friends who have passed from this life,
Or the sick in search of cure,
Or someone with a worried mind,
The strength so we endure.

Somehow this ugly tree became
A symbol of faith and hope,
A chance to ask the Lord for help
And his grace to let us cope.

This little tree thought its work was done,
But God said not so fast,
Rest here on the beach a while,
Giving hope to those that pass.

Armadillo

I grew up in Carolina
And knew all the animals there,
But the only armadillo known
Were the cowboy boots some wear.

I saw the first, here on the farm,
About ten years ago.
Now suddenly they are everywhere,
And how they got here I don't know.

They dig up all the flowers
Planted out there in the yard.
To catch them is near impossible,
Because their head is kind of hard.

Not sure of why they came here—
Maybe it's the weather.
It's not too hot and not too cold,
So maybe they like it better.

I wish that they would go away—
All night they just dig holes,
Searching for the tasty grubs
To fill their troll-like souls.

A possum on a half shell
Is one of their nicknames.
I've even seen them once or twice
In some computer games.

This prehistoric-looking creature
That wreaks havoc where it goes,
As it digs up everything in sight,
With its long and pointy nose,

Now I've finally found a use for them,
In my new armadillo boots,
But I think my boots were female, 'cause
The males chase me in hot pursuit.

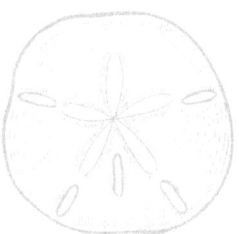

Blackbirds

Blackbirds flying everywhere,
With red upon their wings—
Flocks of hundreds in the air
Predict an early spring.

This time of year, they are coming back
From wherever they went to.
Looks like the weather's warming up
As they are coming into view.

So many on the power line,
They almost make it sway.
I hope that it can stand the strain,
And I pray it don't give way.

They fly with such coordination,
Looking like a darkened cloud,
Every one of them in sequence—
To break formation's not allowed.

Nature's version of Blue Angels,
A phenomenon at its best,
Every wing, in lock step,
Like every bird must pass a test.

They rise and fall and twist and swirl,
And soon they are all gone.
I'm so lucky that I got to see
Them make their way back home.

Sharks

If you play in salty waters,
There's a chance you'll see a shark
It's best if you remember this
If you wish there to embark,

After all, their home's the ocean;
They can travel where they please.
They are free to live and swim around
Throughout the world and seven seas.

They're the apex ocean predator,
Second only to killer whales—
The fear of most good sailors
From any port where they set sail.

But the truth about this creature
Is you're not likely to be its dish;
Your chance of getting bitten
Is far greater from jellyfish.

It's not usually a shark you see
When you look out and see a fin.
Could be a stingray cutting waves
Or just a dolphin now and then.

It's likely that they'll still be here
When we are long since gone,
Just like it's likely they were here
Before humans came along.

Enjoy the day spent at the beach,
With umbrellas and your chair.
No need to fear what you can't see—
Don't be worried; just be aware.

But what's really kind of funny
Is this thing of which we fear
Is likely only to be seen
Printed on all of your beach gear.

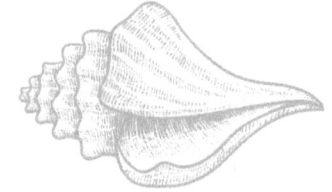

Roseate Spoonbill

You can see God's sense of humor
With the animals he created,
But some may wish to change their look,
Because their nose they've always hated.

The amazing roseate spoonbill,
With its lovely pinkish feathers,
But the match between its head and beak
Don't seem to go together.

Its bill looks kind of awkward,
As if it's been smashed in a door,
Shaped like a spoon for eating soup
And not for critters along the shore.

It feeds in the shallow waters
Of the creeks around the marsh,
One of the prettiest birds I ever seen,
But its beak is kind of harsh.

It seems to get along just fine—
It cares not what others think—
'Cause its beak is really handy
When just trying to get a drink.

But the other day I heard one say,
In strict confidence with a stork,
My beak is great for scooping things,
But at times I'd like a fork.

Tree Frog

How can something so dang small
Produce so loud a noise?
It's like it has a built-in amp,
And it's designed to just annoy.

Some barely over just one inch,
But the whole thing's vocal chords.
The noise this thing can produce
Can shake the nails right out the boards.

It seems to cling to everything
On the outside of my house,
And at night they hold a concert there,
With no way to drown them out.

This little green and sticky frog
Will drive you straight insane,
And Lord have mercy on your soul
When they see it start to rain.

There have been times when overnight
I thought that I would suffocate
With my pillow clamped around my head,
Hoping this noise I could negate.

But over time I have come to learn
There's not much that can be done,
But I swear at times I've had the thought
To chase them with my gun.

Beach Forever Gone (Erosion)

Tree just standing way up high,
Two feet above the land,
Roots that should be under dirt
Run straight down in the sand.

Kind of odd to see this thing,
Standing on a pile of twigs,
But the sea has eaten everything
That once made this a ridge.

All that stands here now is dead,
But this tree just don't know yet,
Slowly eaten by the waves,
Like a silent silhouette.

Tomorrow may be just the day
When it joins up with the rest,
Lying there upon the sand
When the tide begins to crest.

Like something from a movie
About a land that has been lost,
The ocean dines upon the shore,
And tremendous is the cost.

The old front beach has disappeared,
And now it lies far offshore.
The woods that lined this coastal place
Are now gone forevermore.

It hasn't happened overnight,
But just a little day by day.
The sad part is it's not been long,
'Cause I've watched as it decayed.

I don't know what we now can do,
But it will never be the same.
So be sure to visit while you can,
Because this land the sea will claim.

Evenings on the Farm

A couple days throughout the year,
If you're standing there just right,
You can see the moon rise in the east,
While in the west the sun bids good night.

In early spring out on this farm,
Before the trees fill out with leaves,
I can stand just back behind the house
And watch the colors the sky weaves.

"So blessed am I that this I see,"
I stand here lost in thought.
"Is this God's way of showing off,
With the views my eyes have caught?"

The work at times can get you down,
Out here on this little farm,
But the simple little joys abound
In this place so full of charm.

Some things in life make you feel small,
With the burdens we all carry,
But times like these make me so glad
That this place is extraordinary.

God sends to me reminders
This is where my life should be—
Inland just a little bit,
But still close enough to the sea.

Beach Chair

Two beach chairs sitting all alone,
Above the high tide mark.
Seems to be no one around,
And time is approaching dark.

Did they stake their spot for watching stars,
And just walk home to get a drink?
But two beach chairs sitting all alone
Makes one's mind begin to think.

Could they be here just forgotten
Or left for someone else to use?
Or maybe there are secrets here,
As they seem a bit abstruse.

Did they walk off into the ocean,
And never will they return?
Or walked off to pick up seashells,
And no cause for my concern.

Were they swept out by a riptide—
Two lovers holding hands?
It wouldn't be the first time
We've lost someone from these sands.

It could be we will never know,
As so many grace these shores,
But still they leave a mystery
For us to ponder or just ignore.

The Storm's Not Over Yet

The dark outside gives way to light,
Although caution still applies.
Is the storm we weathered finally past,
Or are we caught within its eye?

Huddled in the hallway,
The safest place they say,
I wish we'd not been stubborn
And just drove inland for the day.

I'd love to get a breath of air
And out of this stagnant heat,
'Cause the AC doesn't work so well
When power lines lie on the street.

So, we go outside to get some air,
But as we step out our front door,
Nothing out there looks the same
As it did the day before.

So much destruction just outside—
That's when reality sets right in—
And with the backside of the storm's approach,
We now hunker down again.

The winds begin to blow once more,
And with that comes much more fear,
Because now we've seen what it can do,
And again it's getting near.

We say a prayer and force a smile,
But the tension is there to see.
We keep hoping that it won't be long
Until this storm will let us be.

So, God has blessed us one more time,
And all are safe and sound.
But outside everything's a mess,
With all this storm has blown around.

For weeks to come, we will rebuild,
And I also have a feeling
We'll eat beany weenies for at least a month
And won't be too dang appealing.

Seagulls

Squawk, squawk, squawk, the seagulls talk,
As they call to all their friends.
At first, there's only one or two,
Now like a parade that doesn't end.

Where on earth did they all come from?
My gosh, how they compete.
All after just one tiny fish,
They dive down for a treat.

At times they fly like acrobats,
At times they float on waves,
Sometimes frozen in midair,
When a harsh wind blows their way.

The most beautiful sight to sailors
That have been lost out on the sea,
They're like a vision of an angel
That says land's within their reach.

They've been here since the start of time
In almost every coastal region,
And come rain or shine, they're always out,
No matter what the season.

A pretty bird of black and white
And a big part of the scenery,
Just like the beach, the waves, and sand,
And all the island's greenery.

But unless you want to see firsthand
How many you can get to screech,
The best advice that I can give
Is don't eat popcorn out on the beach.

Clearing Land

The peaceful sounds of morning
Are replaced with a clickety clack,
Drowning out the songbird's song
With the sound of the track-hoe tracks.

The smell of springtime flowers,
Now replaced by smell of smoke,
As the burn pile is getting larger
Out in the middle of the oaks.

This morning what was a forest
By afternoon it becomes a field.
What started inside an office
By those that seal the deals.

More houses must be needed
Along this rural route.
Progress dictates that man came first,
So the animals must move out.

Trees that stood a hundred years
Are now on their way to mill.
Soon you'll see the roads appear,
As the builders show their skill.

It's a vicious little cycle,
As people move to this locale
And destroy the beauty that brought them here,
So I don't see the rationale.

And I am just as guilty—
I built my farm out in this place
To raise my little family
Far from the city's pace.

I don't have all the answers,
But I sure don't like the view
As the city's moving closer
And appears like overnight it grew.

Power of Water

Water drops can cut a hole
Into the hardest rock
Or power entire cities
As it flows through hydrolocks.

It can float the mighty cargo ships
Stranded on the raging sea
And hide, so far within its depths,
Things man will never see.

It can frost the tops of mountains
Or cool the desert sands,
Make rivers swell beyond their banks,
Wreaking havoc across the land.

It can reduce to bits of rubble
Things built by mortal man
In efforts to control its flow
When it doesn't fit within their plans.

But it can also be as gentle
As a snowflake caught on tongue
Or in a peaceful springtime shower
That brings forth flowers when it is done.

Giving life to all it touches,
Without it there's no mankind.
How quickly we would turn to dust
And all life would soon decline.

The most abundant thing on planet earth,
Yet it strains your mind to think,
There are people out there searching
For just a cup, or two, to drink.

The Beauty of Broken Things

A battered ship sinks down below,
Now to the ocean floor it clings.
The creatures there that call it home
Find the beauty in broken things.

The mighty oak lies split in half
By the storms that came last spring.
A fox's den now dug beneath
Shows beauty in broken things.

The old farm fence that used to hold
On to all a farmer's dreams,
But honeysuckle now lays claim
And adds beauty to broken things.

A seashell found along the shore,
Broken by the sea it seems,
Now finds its home on a windowsill,
Due to the beauty of broken things.

An old, rusted truck sits up on blocks,
With its share of dents and dings,
But to a teenage boy that wants to drive,
He sees the beauty in broken things.

A heart that's broken up by tears,
Left with all the pain that brings,
Can find a way to love again,
'Cause there's still beauty in broken things.

Frosty Beach

Most people love to walk the beach
When the warm air blows on shore,
And I must admit, I love it, too,
But there's a time that I like more.

When it's a bit too cool to wear just shorts
And the cold wind passes through,
That's when I love the beach the most—
It's just a different kind of view.

You're mostly out here all alone,
Except for other hard-core locals
That find this place is at its best
Without all the summer vocals.

The sounds you hear are just the ones
Made by birds and winter waves,
And occasionally the sound that's made
When the dolphins come to play.

The peacefulness gets in your soul
And lets your mind slow down to think.
The shorter days and winter haze
Pass by within a blink.

The sea gives up is bounty then,
And there's so few to pick it up—
A million different wondrous things,
As the ocean floor disrupts.

Now some would say I'm crazy,
Out here in my hat and coat,
Barefoot on this frosty beach,
And with my flip-flops that I tote.